Call *of the* Trees

Also by Dorothy Maclean

The Living Silence

Wisdoms

To Hear the Angels Sing

The Soul of Canada

To Honor the Earth

Choices of Love

Seeds of Inspiration

Call *of the* Trees

Dorothy Maclean

The Lorian Association
PO Box 1368
Issaquah, WA 98027
www.lorian.org

Call of the Trees

Photographs by Alan Watson,
Brian Ziegler and Jeremy Berg

Cover photograph from www.istockphotos.com

Edited by Freya Secrest

Published by The Lorian Association
PO Box 1368
Issaquah, WA 98027

ISBN 0-936878-13-4

Maclean, Dorothy
Call of the Trees / Dorothy Maclean

Library of Congress Control Number: 2006920181

First Edition: March 2006

Printed in the United States of America

0 9 8 7 6 5 4 3 2 1

www.lorian.org

*This book is dedicated to the fellowship
between
God, Humans and Nature*

Contents

List of Photographs

Note: Intials signify Alan Watson (AW), Brian Ziegler (BZ),
Jeremy Berg (JB), and Dorothy Maclean (DM)

Foreword

Englishman Richard St. Barbe Baker, 1889-1982, conservationist, forester, founder of the "Men of the Trees," was one of the pioneers of ecological forestry and Earth healing. St. Barbe was responsible for planting and inspiring the planting of countless trees worldwide during his lifetime and authored many books. He wrote the following foreword for the first publication of the early tree messages in 1969.

"It is a privilege and pleasure for me to commend these tree messages, lovingly interpreted through Dorothy Maclean of the Findhorn Trust.

"Men of the Trees, dedicated to handing on our tree heritage for others to enjoy, often find that they gain inspiration for their loving service. As they become planters of trees, their own lives are enriched beyond all expectation, for whole communities of trees radiate gratitude and return the love showered on them at compound interest. ... When planting is done in the spirit of worship, a miracle happens.

"The tree messages reveal the occult explanation that scientific research has been unable to give. The ancients believed that the Earth itself is a sentient being and feels the behavior of mankind upon it. As we have no scientific proof to the contrary, I submit that we should accept this and behave accordingly and thus open up for ourselves a new world of understanding.

"How dull life would be if we did not accept anything we could not explain! For my part, I would rather be a believer than an unbeliever. It would be conceited to be otherwise, when there is the miracle of sunrise and sunset in the Sahara, the miracle of growth from the tiny germinating seed to the forest giant - a veritable citadel in itself providing food and shelter for myriads of tiny things which acts as an indispensable link in the Nature cycle and gives the breath of life to man.

"Let us accept that miracle of growth as fact and as a living symbol of the Tree of Humanity and the Oneness of Mankind and all living things.

"Each one of the following messages of Dorothy must be studied separately and taken into the silence of our hearts."

Preface

In September 2002, Vermont Family Forests (VFF) of Bristol, Vermont invited Dorothy Maclean to come to Vermont to share her rare messages from the trees, and to address a pressing question: what is the relationship between humans and the trees?

Her messages alarmed us: they call on humanity to protect the old-growth trees and to re-forest the Earth for its own survival. Motivated by the urgency and timeliness of their call, we made a commitment to each other and to Dorothy to print her tree messages and to broadcast them far and wide like seeds.

None too soon. Three-quarters of the Earth's original forests have been cut. In the meantime, industry is rapidly logging the Earth's remaining tropical and northern forests. Researchers are even now experimenting with the planting of sterile genetically-engineered trees.

VFF is a learning organization which was founded in 1995 to explore and develop new models of forestry that are community-based and ecologically sustainable. After many years of research, VFF found that our dialogue about the forest was invariably one-sided: how could we get beyond the limited, self-interest of our human point of view? If only the trees could speak!

So a group of us invited Dorothy to VFF to share the extraordinary tree messages she has received since 1965. They call us to wake up from our self-absorption and to remember who we really are. Like elders encouraging a young adult to grow up and come into its maturity, the trees urge us to evolve a new relationship with nature.

We learned that the trees are not only the guardians, but also the skin of the Earth. Nature is not a blind crude force but an intelligent presence that is not only able but eager to communicate and cooperate with an awakened humanity. The trees are calling us home to ourselves and to the work of restoring our planet.

We honor Dorothy for her pioneering life work of sharing these profound messages with people all around the world and helping them attune to the truth within. We are touched by her humility and pragmatism and give thanks to her generosity and faith in us.

If these messages from the trees speak to you, then please pass them on. In their words, "we say that you can render the greatest of

iii

services by recognizing us and bringing our reality to human consciousness." Share them with your relatives and friends and network with us at www.callofthetrees.com.

Thank you!

Jonathan Corcoran
Bunny Daubner
Jennifer Vyhnak

Acknowledgements

These tree messages are being published together for the first time. For those being reprinted, we wish to express our appreciation to the Findhorn Foundation, to Lindisfarne Books who published "To Hear the Angels Sing" and "Choices of Love," and to all others who have helped bring these messages into public view.

Special thanks and acknowledgments to Alan Watson, founder of "Trees for Life," and Brian Ziegler for the generous use of their beautiful photographs.

Introduction

The contents of this book put forward a perspective on trees that is not normally presented, and I should like to go into its history, albeit very briefly.

I, a Canadian, came to Britain to do work in World War II. There I met my colleagues, Peter and Eileen Caddy who, like me, were seeking to find the answers as to the purpose of life. Though we had come from different backgrounds, we had each experienced that we were part of a loving universe and could individually get the answers we needed from our inner divinity or intuition.

This knowledge changed us and expanded our capabilities. In 1954 I began daily inner attunements or meditations, putting the loving wisdom of this connection into words. For years, Peter, Eileen and I based our lives on our inner contacts and proved the reality and validity of what we received from that source. For five years, through the use of our guidance for relevant answers to our practical, daily problems, we ran Cluny Hill Hotel in Scotland, bringing it from a financial failure to becoming a popular and successful hotel.

In 1962 we found ourselves living in a trailer park without formal jobs. Knowing from our guidance that it was right to stay there, we augmented our food supply by growing vegetables in the sand surrounding the trailer. The results were pretty miserable, and one morning I received the following from my inner divinity:

"To those who have an insight into life everything has meaning. The forces of nature are something to be felt into, to be stretched out to, and one of the jobs for you is to feel into the nature forces such as the wind, feel its essence and purpose for Me, and be positive and harmonize with that essence.

"It will not be as difficult as you immediately imagine. All the forces are to be felt into, even the sun, the moon, the sea, the trees, the very grass. All are part of My life. All is One life. Humanity, instead of building a generous cooperation with My One life on this planet, has hacked it into pieces. Play your part in making life One again, with My help.

"Begin by thinking about the higher nature spirits, the angels who overlight, and by tuning into them. It will be so unusual to draw their

1

interest here. They will be overjoyed to help and to find some members of the human race eager for their help. By the higher nature spirits I do not mean just the ones that geographically overlight the area but the spirits of the different physical forms such as the spirits of the clouds, of rain, of the separate vegetables.

"In the New World their realms will be quite open to humans – or I should say, humans will be open to them – and when rain is needed, for example, it will be brought about. It is even possible with you now if your faith were great enough and if there were no sense of limitation.

"Now just be open and seek out into the glorious realms of nature with sympathy and understanding, knowing these beings are of the Light, willing to help but suspicious of humans and on the look-out for the false, the snags. Keep with Me and they will find none, and you will build towards the new."

I wondered about this guidance and was very skeptical about pursuing it. Eventually I did follow this instruction, first entering an inner attunement and then focusing on the form and energy of a garden pea, a favorite vegetable that we were growing. To my surprise I made an immediate link and received a creative, helpful response. This began the wonderful experiment in co-operation with the intelligences in nature in the Findhorn Garden. I was helped to understand the process by the following inner message, "You are pioneering in the true attitude to nature, to the One life. For this attitude it behooves you to think of everything in terms of life force – not merely an impersonal force like electricity, but as a manifestation of some being. Not only that, the beings behind the various manifestations are conscious representatives of Me. They can teach you and help you, though what you see of them outwardly may be a lowly bee, a leaf, or a stone. Behind all is a great chain of life, leading to Me. Humans have been given dominion over all these on Earth, but only as you, too, fit into the great chain of life."

At another time my inner guidance related, "I talk of the one world and the interrelation between all life, but there has to be effort to reach into this new conception. It is new, newer than you think. ... The old ties are built up on the conception of each of you as being a separate entity related to other entities. The new ties are built on the conception of you being part of the greater with no separate life. There is a clear distinction between these two.

"Relationships in the old were rather like two dead ends being connected, for, once established, they were inclined to stay static and not grow. In the New, each relationship is living, changing, and new. This in itself takes effort. Nothing can be taken for granted. Always, there has to be an opening out and reaching for further horizons."

From these inner dimensions or soul level of the various species, I asked and received answers to our gardening problems. With this help, our vegetables were astonishingly healthy and our garden eventually drew many visitors, some of whom were interested enough in our spiritual approach to join us. This experiment in co-operating with the intelligence of nature was so successful that we eventually became known as the Findhorn Foundation, now almost forty-five years old.

I realized that the "higher intelligent energies" in nature, the angels or devas (deva is the Sanskrit word for "shining one"), hold the archetypal pattern of form, and the energies known as elementals (energies of earth, air, fire and water) deal more specifically with the physical form. The angels are beyond polarity and hold the most exact, precise and minute forms of nature at all times. Yet they are formless fields of intelligent energy. They are limitless, free and insubstantial. They are responsible, under God, for the perfection we behold throughout the planet, the wonderful exactness of all physical form. This they do in joy and without free will, for they are the great Servers of Life; none of us would exist without their selfless service and that of the various members of their worlds.

I was told, "Do you know that the very thought of mankind about a plant makes contact with the nature world? It is not a great contact and it is not lasting but, nevertheless, humans in their thought world have crossed into our world. ... When we talk about One world, it is reality, not idle talk. You, humanity, may know nothing whatsoever about this, but that does not make it any less true or unreal. If you realized just how much your thoughts impinged on others and on other worlds, you might be more careful, for your thoughts are indeed far-reaching. Every thought has an influence, for it is life-moving, and how seldom it moves in a constructive direction! Blessed are the pure in thought – and powerful too!"

Of course, trees and the nature world don't talk, not as we humans understand talk. In my times of contact I do not hear words, but convey the meaning of my experiences in my own words. The messages contained herein do not come from the spirit of individual trees or any nature form, but from the over-all guiding soul of each species.

The most powerful and urgent message that I received from all of nature was from a tree, the Monterey Cypress, in 1967. [pg. 18] It impacted me so strongly that I felt helpless, for no one around me understood the urgency that it imparted until I met St. Barbe in 1969 and he suggested the publication of the tree messages. Since then, as I have traveled around the globe, I have always tried to share the message of the mature trees in my workshops. While the ecological role of trees is more commonly understood today, the spiritual role of trees has not yet been fully realized. The angels emphasize various reasons for the need for mature trees on the planet. Although they do not agree with our thoughtless approach to trees, they offer us continual love. There was always a sense of friendliness and equality throughout my contact with them.

This book brings together my tree messages, including some shrubs, and is offered in chronological order as they were received. You will notice repetition. Evidently I needed it, needed to be continually told of the love that creates and serves all life. The repetition has not been eliminated, and allows each tree or shrub to communicate the fullness of its message to us humans.

As the Ponderosa Pine Deva once told me: "Face it, you know you are to write about us, and share our togetherness and what we have told you. So spend time writing, getting your thoughts down. Use more paper! Come to us for inspiration!"

As well as thanking the Ponderosa Pine Deva for its creative kick, I want to particularly thank Call of the Trees of Bristol, Vermont, for their initiative and help in getting the message of the trees out to a wider audience.

Each one of us has the capacity to tune into these angelic realms. As they put it to me: "Just tune into nature until you feel the love flow. That is your arrow into the deva world. It does not matter if there is a message or not, it is the state which counts. Always it is your state that the nature world responds to, not what you say, not what you do, but what you are."

4

I hope these messages can inspire and support you to play an ever deeper part in helping our planet.

The first message shown came before the inner contact with nature began, and throughout this book I use the word "God" to describe the life force within all life. My wording was naturally the common language of the day, for instance sometimes referring to God as Father/Mother and myself as a child, because in the interior vastness, so deep and clear, I seemed to be a very small child.

Dorothy Maclean

God Speaks on Trees

The trees are there for you, humanity, trees made by Love for the children of Love. All nature was created for the edification of an ever more perfect creation – including you, My children.

You were also created to create and you have done that, but without the aid of My wisdom. To feed the greed of your disconnected minds you have uprooted forests, you have made scarcity in lands of plenty, because you have created away from Love.

The fate of the trees and all that grow on this earth remain for you to choose, according to whether you are close to your separated selves or close to Me. You may, with all your God-given powers, comply with nature and hasten the growth of the perfect, or you may follow the dictates of the separated mind into an earth denuded and bare.

Recognize quickly your all-comprehensive ignorance and turn to Me, to the source of all knowledge, who is Love and who loves you beyond measure - and all nature will be turned to My Love and will blossom in quite a new way, for the earth will be cleansed. Turn innocently to Love always, to the Love that loves all things.

This was an early message before there was any nature contact.

Landscape Angel

The angel overlighting the planetary work done at Findhorn

Your love for our kingdom joins us to humans. You see, there are no individual egos with us. When you love one beech tree, for example, you love all beech trees, you are connected with the whole genus of beech.

Even though it may be one particular specimen that brings out the love in you, that specimen is incapable of taking your regard to itself, and thus you are automatically linked up with the soul of that species. If the human kingdom could learn this quality, it would mean the end of war and rivalry, competition and strife.

Scots Pine

You had no difficulty in contacting me, owing to your sympathy with trees. We should like to have an area of our own here, but the scope has not yet been given to us. I speak for my brothers in mentioning that contact with any of us, whenever there is opportunity, will be greatly welcome. We have so much to give to humans, if they would only relax in us, and great healing power is ours for you to turn to. We are guardians of the earth in many ways and humans should be part of what we guard. We bid a fond farewell.

Yesterday, I said that contact with any of us would be welcome and, as you can sense, there are many of us here now who would like the contact and who are just tuning in tonight. We are not active young things; we are, in a way, like a school of benevolent philosophers, with inhuman purity and a great wish to serve humanity. Trees are so vital to man and to life on this planet that some of us are eager to experience this new contact, before other humans destroy what we have built up.

Gorse

We stand as guardians of the dunes, guardians of encroaching waste, with roots deep in the earth, and scent and color broadcast. We keep vigil on this plane, with prickles to keep out outsiders. Some plants have a higher function; we are on the lowest – and yet do we not reach to the highest in this our glory? We adorn the desert, we transmute this barrenness. We lift it to the heights and yet at the same time we stay spanning all levels, one of God's most useful creations. Normally you are transported by our golden glory; today we show you another side of our nature, and still we keep the oneness which is the nature of all life. Few keep it and shout it from every blaze of flower on every side.

The sun comes out, and immediately we lighten and lift the contact. You feel now the ripples of golden light coursing out in continuous waves, feel it touch and transform the air, feel it run through your mind and your heart and bring tears of gladness to your eyes. Feel the essential gorse-ness of us, which is God-ness. Always you have this message to spread if you stop, listen and hear. You seldom stop and listen, though you hear us calling, calling over the moors straight to all open hearts. The strength of that call is almost overpowering; we are glad you answered it, for it is God the Highest calling. Make no division; glory in God, glory particularly in us in season. The fact that we touch your heart binds our kingdoms together – and we as guardians and transformers should be one in our purposes, for there is a world to be saved.

We are torn and ground to dust as humans machine us out of the way. We are untouched by this, but it is not right. We are as much part of Divine life as humanity, and while we must keep apart in our waste places, when we and humans meet, there should be communion and a sharing of intention. No part of creation should be taken for granted.

You wonder if you are merely writing down your own thoughts, if we would really speak in this vein. Why should we not? All is not sweetness and light in this world, and there is much that humans can learn from the plant kingdom, particularly from the intelligent beings responsible for this kingdom. Do not deny our voice. Do not expect it to always be or say the same thing. Sense behind me the Landscape Angel, and higher and higher hosts in direct line of ascent to the Highest. They have much to do with this world, quite as much as humans, and yet as you use the results of their doing, how often do you acknowledge or consult or thank any of us? This becomes more and more urgent as more and more of the earth is despoiled. Yes, despoiled.

You know the joy and delight of our kingdom; we share it gladly with you and with everyone, but you must recognize that we too are part of the One Life and that you cannot continue to only take from, never giving, or give for your own selfish purposes. You humans must think in larger terms. You must think of the whole of the Earth, not mine and undermine and give so little. You should be helping the mineral, vegetable and animal kingdoms, not using them.

We know you know this. Nevertheless let us repeat it, for it is important, and who knows who will listen. You are a listening ear, and we have this to say. So we say it, and hope that you may pass it on to those who will not listen directly. Our realms have much of consciousness to pass on.

You look at the wonder and beauty of our blossoms, and marvel that limited plants could communicate in this way. You forget that we are part of the One Life. We do our bit in bringing heaven down to earth, and we would have you do the same. There is much to be done; join us in the one Whole of all life.

Beech

When you are receptive to us, it is as if you are part of our forces; you blend in and you like it and we like it. When you are not so tuned, you are cut off and there is no contact between us. We send a blessing in this rare contact. We bless all who come within our influence, but generally it falls on barren ground. Still, we pour our blessing down in everlasting benediction, unmoved, as you come and go your various ways. Your reception repays us a hundred-fold and we give thanks to our Creator.

Tree Devas

Most certainly you can contact us from a distance. Distance is nothing with the faculties used in this exchange. One reason you feel our influences more strongly than that of other types of plants is that we have stayed in our places through the years, through the centuries sometimes, and have thereby created a strong atmosphere, as we reach up high, like lightning rods, to attract the forces. Our auras are so steady and peaceful that restless humans find blessings in us. We have not a sense of self; we do not grasp and thrust for ourselves. Remember, we can talk to you and open up other One-world secrets as you open yourselves to us.

Tree Devas

There is a great crowd of us here, exulting that you have planted trees in the garden and opened up so much by so doing. Our forces, grounded here, will make a great deal of difference to the balance of the whole and, although time seems needed, we shall all advance as much as possible. We need a fully grown tree for our real influence - a child cannot do what a man can do - but we think that, with our concentration and your co-operation, we can make the influence strong soon. Anyway, we are absolutely delighted with today's developments and your quick action. We look forward to a long and happy co-operation.

Tree Devas

Our forces are being anchored here, if only as a small beginning, and they also link you more with the neighboring property. We are glad of that! It makes it easier to grow trees when there are others near. We are very anxious for our influence to be with you, and are concentrating on this. You can give us strength by your thoughts and by thinking of the little trees as larger and stronger than they are.

Monterey Cypress

We are not just the little trees you see in your garden. We are denizens of the magnificent spaces of great hills in the sun and wind. We put up with being hedges, but always in our inner being is a growing towards the open, sun-kissed places where we stand out in clustered grandeur.

You feel in us an almost intolerable longing to be fully ourselves. We of the plant world have our pattern and our destiny, worked out through the ages, and we feel it is quite wrong that we and others like us are not allowed to be, because of humanity and its encroachment. Trees are not so much Do-ers of the Word as Be-ers. We have our portions of the plan to fulfill; we have been nurtured for this very reason and now, in this day and age, many of us can only dream of the spaces where we can fulfill ourselves. The pattern is ever before us, out of reach, a dream we are forever growing towards but which seldom becomes reality. The planet needs the like of us in our full maturity. We are not a mistake on the part of nature; we have work to do.

Humanity is now becoming controller of the world forests and is beginning to realize that these are needed, but you use silly economic reasons for your selection with no awareness of the planet's needs. You should not cover acres with one quick-growing species which, though admittedly better than none, shows utter ignorance of the purpose of trees and their channeling of diverse forces. The world needs us on a large scale. Perhaps if you were in tune with the Infinite, as we are, and were pulling your weight, the forces would be balanced, but at present the planet needs more than ever just what it is destroying – the very forces which go through the lordly trees.

We have been vehement. Here are these facts of life forever with us and with no one to listen to them. We have rather dumped this on you. Though you feel at one with us, you feel unable to help. You are only looking at it from a limited level. We know that the very telling of this to you does help, that a truth once in human consciousness then percolates around and does its work. And we feel the better for communicating!

Let us both believe that the Almighty One knows all this better than either of us and that something is being done.

Horse Chestnut

We are most impressed by your little corner of the world, by the welcoming spirit. You see, although humans have been given dominion over the earth and have arranged and planned gardens, often very admirable ones, of late this has been done with no awareness of the divine life as expressed through our kingdoms. You have therefore cut yourselves off from a very large chunk of life. That is why wild places untouched by humanity have a magic and vitality lacking in the most beautiful man-made garden. That is why you, for example, much prefer the wild places, however barren they may be, for there we can be in fullness without the curtailing consciousness of people. We can be free, where humanity has not thought inharmoniously, and can find healing there.

Here we hope to pioneer a new garden where we may be in fullness because humans recognize and co-operate with us. Much will have to be worked out, but given the right attitudes we believe something may be evolved. You have already noticed the unusual growth in this tree, made possible through your attitudes.

Always we create for you the clear high purity of our realms. Partake of it; humanity has much need of it.

Later, when this tree was moved, it did not grow as well as in its previous position.

As you know, we joined in the joy of the move and were grateful for all the solicitude shown.

One of the reasons that this tree thrived so much in its previous position was that you were all continually passing, admiring and blessing it. In its present position it is out of the way and, if it is to thrive equally here, you will have to go out of our way to pass it and give it love. We of course will play our part in caring for it, and hope you will do the same.

Laburnum

We are another part of plant life eager to contact you, a part much used to human contact of the usual kind. When we burst forth at this time of the year with our yellow shower, we give out ourselves and we receive human appreciation. Then for the rest of the year we are on our own again.

You can feel the tumbled generosity of our giving, of our way of expressing ourselves, exquisite down to each perfect shaping. The pattern is there with nothing in us to stop it, and you wish you were as free and able to be true to your pattern and express it as we are. We are what we are with no complications such as in your world; in one way we even consider it a diversion to "talk" now on such things as complications, for we are life to be expressed and are very busy expressing it now. The flow is there going out, channeled, on and on. While letting that flow go on, with one corner of ourselves we talk, but you would find us very different if you tuned in to us at a different time of the year when our forces are focused in another direction. Perhaps you will, but now is the time we are most truly expressing ourselves, expressing God's wonderful abundance and endless flowing vitality.

Of course the little transplanted tree in the garden is behind. The vitality cannot flow normally until properly connected up with its environment. This expressing force you feel is but one of many, for nothing is independent; all are related and transplanting brings many adjustments. You can help it best at present by seeing it as perfect, holding strongly to the idea of its perfection can very much aid it to conform to its pattern, for when the pattern is strong enough, physical lacks can be overcome as is being evidenced in your garden.

It is quite difficult to touch into your thinking mind when this beautiful flow of force calls us. We now go fully into it. Enter in also, any time, and be free with us and in harmony with all.

Rhododendron

Vivid and somber, sunshine and rain, and over all a great love for being, a tenacity and exclusiveness. We settle in wherever we can, and get down to the business of being. We thank you for bringing us into the garden; we thank all who have allowed us roothold and life throughout the country, for we do like to settle.

Each species contributes something to the character of the land, and changes it. Just as you in your human evolution are now moving out of functioning as separate individuals or separate specialized groups, so is the plant world changing and the flora becoming less specialized and more typical of the whole earth.

Link with us whenever and wherever you see us. This is good for us and good for our relationship. Notice us, see us with new eyes, notice the way we grow. It will help you to imbibe the unique quality which we bring. All are part of the whole, but interest is in the diversity of the parts. The philosophy and the plant life of a country are more related than you might think. Now that greater world unity is coming, let us not lose the essence of each unique contribution.

We shower you with ourselves in the greatest friendliness, and look forward to closer links.

Scots Pine

You feel our gladness and harmony in just being; we are guardians in the sunshine over our allotted land. Like you, each individual tree is affected by conditions, and on a perfect day exudes more of itself than when the weather makes it creep into itself.

We thank humanity for planting us so extensively and enabling us to reclaim much territory. You see, trees act as a protective skin to the Earth and in that skin bring about necessary changes. We are outer sentinels of that change, able to do our work where others could not tread. We glory in this; our high praise goes forth from us like the scent from a flower. It blesses all who come into our aura and rest, but our life is not felt consciously by those of you who are so self-absorbed that you are closed to our qualities. Nevertheless, all are influenced on certain levels; you cannot come into our forests without part of you synchronizing with that range which is common to us both.

You, humanity, are part of all life, physically being the culmination or apex of Earth manifestation, and there is that in you which harmonizes with all life on Earth. We trees, rooted guardians of the surface, converters of the higher forces to Earth through to the ground, have a special gift for you in this day and age of speed and drive and busyness. We are calm strength, endurance, praise, fine attunement, all of which are greatly needed in the world.

We are all more than that. We are expressions of the Love of the Creator for the planet's abundant, unique and related life. We all have purpose; we could not do without one another, however isolated or self-sufficient we may be geographically. The whole of life is here and now, and it is our privilege to breathe out our note of it. Come to our side whenever you can, lift up your consciousness and whisper with us to the wind and the light that all is well outwardly, inwardly and in a thousand directions and to a thousand finer unknown levels here and now, for life is. All is One, that only One.

Southernwood

Whether it rains or the sun shines, whether the wind blows or all is peace, makes no difference to our contact. Although the outer forms may be affected, the controlling consciousness behind is undisturbed and as you remain calm in any storm, you link up with and control all worlds. We do not fly into emotional storms, however provoked by humans or other influences, and therefore our patterns, as expressed in the plant world, come through in perfection. So too will your purposes come through in perfection when you hold clearly to them, undeterred by outer events. This cannot but happen; it is law, the creative power given to you and given to us to wield.

There is chaos in the human world because every wind of chance is likely to influence you, and you are not conscious of, or do not hold to your purpose. When you do, you are creative masters of the world, our brothers, ready to meet the changes which are part of life.

If the pattern that you call southernwood has served its purpose and is to be no more, so be it. Consciousness moves on, life is ever richer, all is gain. Patterns are bound to change as life unfolds. We all learn and grow and express what we are meant to express. The consciousness behind the rhythms of life that you call birth and death on various levels in various timings goes on.

Continuity of consciousness is peace. When storms cut you off from yourselves, you lose peace. In the most intense activity can be peace, because you are one with your plan and purpose, one with the life which you are, single, not a multiplicity of cross currents. The oblivion of sleep is not peace, though it brings its own blessing. We always know what we have to do and therefore have peace, and the joy of the doing.

As our worlds merge more, you too will have to find a single consciousness, the God within you. Then, though the outside worlds erupt and explode, God's patterns will manifest and, through consciousness, all worlds and any form will carry the perfect pattern. Together this is our work, and in joy it is done. Praise God.

Cedar of Lebanon

Peace is what we give you at the moment. You humans are all of a dither with new energies, and we would counterbalance you. Find peace and stability and build on it. It is no use building on foundations that would crumble; it is no use building on wonderful new ideas unless you can ground them. We do not mean that they should be grounded on the old ideas, but on the inner peace and stability deep within. As you take some action without, there should be more action within - in fact, the within should come first, and the trouble with so many humans is that this is not done. See how our enormous limbs are balanced in peace. When the storm comes, we go with it and keep the balance.

The mind world of humanity is bursting its seams. Let it burst. Many ideas will be bubbles that will come to nothingness. That does not matter; keep your roots in peace, and experiment. Experiment until you find that which comes through perfectly. As a baby learns to walk, learn to walk in your new world with a conscious link to peace within. This is our particular message now.

Tree Devas

You are in a place [Findhorn] without large trees and they therefore do not come into your feelings. This cannot be helped at the moment, but we would emphasize the absolute necessity to have large trees for the well-being of the land. The control of such things as rainfall is often in our hands, but as well we draw forth inner radiances, which are as necessary to the land as rain. Because we know of the importance of your scheme and of what we can give to it, we are lending our forces here, although there are no trees. This will have a certain effect, and we can also be drawn by love from any of you. So let us come into your heart now and again, and perhaps, some time, we will find our way into your land.

Gorse

We welcome you. Where no one else could welcome you, we surround you with ourselves in the glory of the open spaces. We come and we blend life in the shunned space, filling the air with our perfume and the hillocks with our gold. And we bask, and go on basking.

In peace we think of the range we cover: from high up where our pattern was conceived and nurtured, down to our manifesting that pattern out of air, sand, water and warmth, out of the innermost realm of ideas to form in the waste lands, out of nothingness to the perfection of each glowing petal. The sun shines on us; we could do nothing without it. We are one with it, you are one with it. It is our heart, not just the light of the day and the warmth of every vein, but the intelligent Giver of all.

Yes, any of our hosts can and do enter this dell. Is not every sound true and worshipful, with nothing to mar and jar the perfection? Of course the angels may enter anywhere, but when human consciousness is aware of disharmony through the ears, the eyes, the nose, our presence is kept at bay and rendered futile. Here we are close, here you can come and get back to Source with all the senses on all levels of consciousness, for here we are ourselves. Here the links between us and our Maker are more evident to you.

For us those links are never marred. We see, we know, we feel our oneness with the earth, water, heat, air and spirit. We are them, every pore of us on every level. We know humans are blind to this and distracted from it, though this oneness is obviously what life is. We do not drink in these qualities and feel separate from them; we are these qualities, part of the whole. That sun out in the sky is not separate; it is part of our being, incorporated. It glows on us, we glow on it.

Whence comes our color? We extract the most from the elements and show forth our wisdom, light and shining, warm and complete, yet shy and wild. Could any other colors say this? Light is donned in contrast to the somberness and tautness necessary to maintain our life in the relatively less lush lands. We are of God; we prove it as we blossom.

Take our essence with you as you go into your unreal worlds of strange values. Remember that we are whole and complete, that you are whole and complete, and let us always remind you of that.

Bamboo

I come in an instant. I conjure up in your mind an essence of the East, of what bamboo means to you, and then you realize that lovely as that essence may be it is but man-made, and that I am Spirit, free and of God. I am Spirit come to manifest here in the garden where you have given me a charge. The conditions are not natural, but the intelligence and force-field (which is kin to Love) which I am, is implanting itself here now to establish an aura, a vibration which will be unaffected by atmosphere. I am grounding myself, making myself what I am in that small corner.

You would help that grounding. Salute it whenever you pass or think of it, and so further establish it. Of course, help with conditions on the physical level as much as you can, but above all aid in the consciousness of bamboo being there. Let that consciousness be guided by what you see, fortifying those particular leaves, that particular stem. Help me be. This is the helpful approach at the moment, delineating the lines of force as I am doing.

Another time when you see the bamboo, it may be that another process is going on. Therefore be sensitive and ready to pick up the need of that moment. Nature – and indeed all creation – expresses itself on all levels: in the color, the shape, the texture, the direction of every leaf, but above all and containing all, is that wonderful combined "feel" which I am, my note which I would sound strongly here. Let that be your concentration, for it is of the Spirit and permeates all levels. That established, I can be, I can express and contribute. This is important here, and it is important that we talk as we do, rise up and soar to the highest heavens, to the one Source of All, and bow in gratitude together, together, together.

Lombardy Poplar

We are glad to ground ourselves in this garden. We would wish for warm sunshine – we shall have to make a plea on behalf of many of us to the weather gods to be kind to us here! Oh yes, this is possible: "Ask and ye shall receive." All things are possible when done to the glory of God. Humans discover the laws by which weather changes happen and now attempt to forecast these changes, but our world of intelligent being is the instrument used to implement the laws. The garden here is already protected to a certain extent as it works with Divine law; more can be achieved. But this is not my field and I only mention it because you brought up the subject yourself by remembering me strongly in connection with heat.

You know me, tall and stalwart, leaves delicately fluttering and shining, part of the scheme of things. So was I made, and so I hope to continue in delight. You can sense the joy of being, of being just as I am and growing ever more so.

You need our help in the garden, but we need your help to be ourselves in the conditions here. See us, each of us, unique in our place and waxing strong. Love to see us becoming ourselves, and it will help us. Of course when we are established we have the bit between our own teeth, but until then you can help greatly. It is not easy for some of us here; we do ask your aid at this stage. Let your love and our joy mingle together and make the desert bloom to the greater glory of the One who made us all.

Birch

We have known you would come, for the awareness of our essence has been strong in you. The higher you go in appreciation of our nature, the closer you go to the Heart and Mind of Useful Beauty which made us all. In fact it is hard to know where we begin and where the One who created us ends – where does a sunbeam become a sunbeam and not the sun? How could our leaves flutter without the wind, how could our bark shine white without the light, how could we stand upright without the earth to feed and hold us, how could we be watered without the cloud and the sun to make the cloud?

We exult in what we are, for so it is. We rejoice in any consciousness that appreciates what we are, that appreciates the fineness, preciseness and delicacy, the power and patience which culminates in a birch tree. We stand in our positions here, and as we stand we spread what we have to contribute for all to see. We are no accident; we are part of the whole. Each plant species is individual yet part of the whole. Here we are, above unrest, forever one with what we should be. We greet you and trust you will often greet us.

Weeping Willow

Come up into our worlds, up high, almost to a point which contains all life in itself. Here is concentrated stillness and from here radiate plans and patterns. From here, I reach out a long arm to each willow in the world, containing it in the stillness and bathing it with radiance. It becomes a distinct entity on its own but is nevertheless part of the invisible consciousness which I am. From my point of stillness, great ripples of energy go forth. Yes, I am aware of others similarly engaged, but in the center itself the pattern is exclusive as it emanates outward. Yes, I am aware of being contained in the greater Stillness; I am sharing with you this aspect of ourselves, this holy place of Creation. Breathe softly and do not disturb the delicate force lines here at Source.

Like humans, we have many levels of consciousness. Now come with me to the tree in your garden. Feel that same pattern grounded and insisting on being. The response and alignment is not one hundred percent as it is not an established tree, but we persevere and will make it so. The tree consciousness is still somewhat fuzzy; give it love, for it has had a jolt and love soothes and smoothes away the complications. Normally it would radiate a settled well-being but that is not yet so.

We have shown you the indomitable side of our natures, the holding of the pattern from the center out to the farthest specimen – farthest in that the response to the lines of force have been tampered with by transplanting. You know we are the freest beings in Creation; we have been showing you how we are also completely bound, so much a part of our work that nothing could separate us.

Yes, humanity interferes as if our results belong to you and, as long as you think this, there will be division between our two worlds. When you recognize your great silent Source, the same for all, then will all fit in and the weeping willow will be perfect in the perfect place everywhere.

Mock Orange

We are here before you think of us; we are always with our plants. We are attached to each little charge because we love to see it grow and have the keenest delight in being part of its development out of nothing into a perfect example of the pattern we hold. Not one little pore is out of line. Out of the elements we carve and unite, and carve again a living example of one design of the Infinite Designer.

And what fun it is! Each little atom is held in its pattern in joy. We see you humans going grayly about your designs, doing things without zest because "they have to be done," and we marvel that your sparkling life could be so filtered down and disguised. Life is abundant joy; each little bite of a caterpillar into a leaf is done with more zest than we sometimes feel in you humans – and a caterpillar has not much consciousness. We would love to shake this sluggishness out of you all to make you see life as ever brighter, more creative, blooming, waxing and waning, eternal and one.

While talking to you, I am also peacefully promoting growth in the plant. All over the world wherever I grow, I hold and confirm the wonderful design of each plant. Maintaining life in countless places, yet I remain free, utterly and completely free, because I am the life of the Lord. And how I rejoice to be alive! I soar to the highest heaven; I become part of the heart of all. I am here, there and everywhere, and I hold my pattern of perfection without deviation. I bubble with life. I am life. I am one; I am many.

I have leapt lightly into your consciousness. I bow out, glad to have been with you, glad that you have appreciated what I have said, and still more glad to go back to our world of light. Think well of us; think of us with light.

Lawson Cypress

You welcome us and we respond. You see us tall and darkly handsome, bringing shade and cover, and such is our function. We will do our best here – and when we say best, we mean best. When humanity can supply our material needs and channel love and light to us, the results will astonish you. We do not mean results merely in terms of size and luxuriance but in the communion, unity and sharing of the One Life passing between us. No child would be afraid of the dark when it knows we are here, and the animals can be particularly playful. All life can go its way – and much of it we make possible by standing erect on the Earth, linking earth with air and sun in an unending and pleased service.

Humanity makes or mars that service, and we suggest that we be mutually creative, mindful of the necessity of the service and promoting it on the widest scale. Vast areas need us – and by "us" I mean mature trees in general. We simply cannot emphasize this enough. We are the skin of this world; take us away and the whole creature can no longer function but dries up and dies. Let us be and the creature purrs with contentment and life goes on, ever moving in natural sequence, more and more benign and more and more and more aware of Unity in the One.

You ask if we glimpse into the future. We are in tune with Life as it should be and therefore, if the future is to be better than the past, we glimpse it. Humanity has made us more conscious of our function by interfering with it and thus good has inadvertently come and, as we said before, together a higher and more perfect world can result. We are glad to add our comment on this; we would have them recorded in all human consciousness if we could.

We send our blessings down. May they be as far-reaching and as fruitful as the shade and cover we would provide, and may the future perfection be soon.

Rowan

We come from the heights, the heights of the spirit and the heights of the land, where we glorify God and bring our scarlet touch of rarified hardiness. We love our open spaces and wild corners, but we gladly come down to this garden to join the others – we would not be left out!

You catch the essence of us all, of all of nature; Heaven brought down to Earth, Earth brought up to Heaven, meeting and manifesting in countless forms and colors, not only to beautify a world but to be part of the life of the world, indispensable, in infinite variety, fulfilling all needs. Each one of us contributes our part in perfection.

Feel the joy with which we play that part. We are what we are, evolved through ageless wisdom, unique in our role, free to rejoice. We sweep into the trees in clouds of joy, while keeping a toehold in the spaces. There is a diminishing portion of the Earth left in its natural state as humanity spreads and spreads. We make a plea to you to be guided in your control of the land, to observe nature's ways, for they are God's ways and have meaning in the whole. Any of us gladly beautify your gardens and produce for your use, although each and every one of us also has a broader use in the world. We are no accident; each tree, shrub and plant has purpose in the overall scheme of things. God's ways are best; tune in to them and the world will return to sanity and joy.

Prunus

We dance into the garden in our spring colors – why should we not be dressed up in our best finery? We bless each of our plants but don't stop at that; we include all in this season of joy. This is our expansive time and we are firmly linked here. We are in many places and cannot envisage it in any other way, for this is spring when we beautify the Earth and call forth delight from all who see us. This is the time when humans of all ages point to us and are glad, when the insects enjoy us, when the sun shines to bring life and the rain comes to hasten it, when the birds sing as never before. This is a time of general rejoicing. We are in a jubilant mood and all cooperate with us; all are lifted out of the ordinary to what is ordinary in our world – the high joy of Life abundant expressing itself now.

Yes, "all" means humans. Human atmosphere is very predominant on Earth; human thoughts and emotions are strongly present influencing many layers of life. Not often do you come into the layer that I am talking from now, which is a great pity because you can, as it is really more your home than the heavy lower levels which so many humans frequent. You humans are out of your depth in the depths where you live; you should be co-creators with us, using the sparkle of life to make perfection as we do. Your powers are equal to ours and more – but what a strange mess you make of them! What a world this would be if you rode high as we do and all of creation were One in the joy of the Lord! How this old/young world would respond and shake off its shackles! We are of this world, but you are too. Let us rejoice together and make it perfect as it should be. Let us be gay and happy. This is the season, now.

Remember us. Don't just file this message of ours away. You are hearing a true voice and every single human has within a voice like ours, uplifting and rejoicing. Listen and act – and thank you.

Lawson Cypress

Our brethren have told you before of the need of the surface of the Earth to have its large trees again; all of us feel this and are very close in response. The planet itself cries out for us in bulk, but humanity, intent on its own devices, goes its way, oblivious. We remain overlighting, ready to play our part as always. We have been so much a part of the destiny of this world and also that of humanity, who has found us indispensable, that we cannot envisage any future unless forests are allowed to come back.

There have always been mighty changes in the past as this Earth has evolved, but always, while the sun shines and life depends on water, our role has been necessary and will continue to be. All of life will change and will be raised, will be lighter and happier and more aware, but nevertheless we still have much to do. We still have our purpose as given to us from on high, and that purpose flows as strongly as ever. We feel it coursing through us in waves of strength straight from Source, and that is why we seize every opportunity to tell you of the need for the forests.

Humanity has control of more and more of the surface of the Earth, and we would reach your mind that you may know, without a doubt, what should be. Your Creator, our Creator, has thought of all things; you have taken on part of your inheritance as a child of God without the wisdom needed to fulfill the role. It is One Life; we come in and proclaim this, attempting to make this clear to you.

What is important now is consciousness. We give praise and thanks that your consciousness and my consciousness meet and blend, that we each know that no part of life can be separated out. Our nature worlds are essential; much of yours, with its false sense of a separate selfhood, is not essential, but together we can cover this Earth with the perfection planned by its Maker.

Golden Conifer

We are happily established here, but are always glad to make the conscious contact, for our intelligence is. We ourselves are very much alive, and unawareness of this fact on the part of humanity seems an inexplicable waste. Why do you go around in little water-tight worlds of your own as if you were the only intelligence, when all around you our world is bursting with awareness, full of the knowledge and truth that the Creator gives us and which would be of inestimable value to you?

Now, for instance, you hear the rain and just consider it as water coming down making a noise and quenching the thirst of plants. You simply accept it as an inanimate thing, or part of a process, and you miss all the joy of the Spirit of Rain with its broad intelligence and great role in all life. You miss that which rain could impart of Oneness and flexibility to change and flow with the life of the Creator in the moment. Rain could be an example for all time and beyond, but you cut out all these mysteries and remain in narrow ruts.

We do not want to have a preaching aura with what we convey; we simply want to share with you and make you realize the abundant, bounding, integrating life which is all around you in our worlds, which is always there and always has been and with which you could be communing to the great betterment of this and every planet. You and I both have the equipment to share and can be joyous together as we each fulfill the roles which the Creator has for us. The same One Life flows in our veins, and the more we recognize and act on this fact, the more will all worlds come together in unison. This coming together is of the plan, for, in truth, we are all children of the One, all part of the One Life, all here because we are meant to be here.

You wonder how awareness of us fits into your everyday living. We can only answer that from our point of view. We see you going around in a world of energy of which you are very much a part, yet closing off your connections with it and concentrating on a minute part of the whole. You have short-circuited yourselves when you could be dynamos of power and great transformers. To us you seem half-dead, when all the time you could spark here and there with all of Life and join in the great, moving, shining whole of it. You are limited. You need not be – and in your limitation you do dreadful things. When your awareness is increased, your life will be completely different – free, unfettered and universal. We are all for you opening out to all of Life, where you will find the One who is never absent, and with us you will praise It forever. Every tree, every atom tells this story, and humans could be aware of it if they would.

We thank you for listening. May our worlds be more and more one in the joy of the One Life.

Landscape Angel

It is good that you feel more clearly the function of large and mature trees as conductors of energy. There they stand, ever ready and channeling the universal forces which surround and are part of the world. Mountains are channels for this energy, especially pointed ones, but the large trees are of a higher and more living substance and are carriers of especially potent vibrations. They are magnificent sentinels for us and for the cosmic energy from the universe. They stand rooted and upraised, transforming the power in an aura of peace.

We repeat again, the large trees are essential for the well-being of the Earth. No other can do the job they do. They and humanity could live in very close harmony and mutual respect, each representing the apex of a particular form of life, and humanity could gain much by association with these trees. It is not for nothing that the Buddha is said to have found enlightenment under a tree. The glory of the open spaces can be focused and concentrated by a great tree and made of use to the Earth.

Let your love go forth to the trees. That they are vanishing all over the world is but another sign of the troubled times at the end of an age. Mature trees are necessary for the welfare of the planet. Hold and broadcast this in thoughts of power, and thank God for their creation.

Tree Devas

You have asked how you can show your gratitude to us for the serenity you have received from us. We say that you can render the greatest of services by recognizing us and bringing our reality to human consciousness. It is a fact that we are many yet speak with one clear voice; it is fact that we are the overlighting intelligence of each species, not the spirit of individual trees. It is fact that we are vitally concerned with the Earth as a whole and, because we see humanity interfering detrimentally with the unit you call this planet, we would communicate with you to make you more aware of God's laws regarding the planet.

Just as humanity has vehicles in various realms and can function in various dimensions, so can we, in a different way, for God is Consciousness itself. Though a tree or a plant may have little consciousness compared to humanity, we are what is behind the growing self-awareness of life. God always needs hands and feet, and we are those hands and feet bringing about those miracles of growth which lead to self-consciousness and then God-consciousness. We are part of your growth in the distant past; we are part of your growth now. As you return to the Source and become its hands and feet, you cannot but be conscious of this life in us, for there is nothing which is not of God. And the more you recognize our role and act accordingly, the better for all life on this Earth and elsewhere.

Humanity, as a whole, has no awareness of us. You can ground this recognition strongly and bring us into human consciousness, which is very necessary for any progress on Earth. Nature – and your body is part of nature – is not a blind force. It is conscious and maneuverable. It has inner vehicles just as you have.

We are of the truth, we exist. Therefore, you who are coming to truth will recognize us with your higher mind in spite of your intellect. Then God's purposes through us both will not be diverted. We are grateful for any spreading of this truth; nothing can be of more value to us. We give of ourselves, of what God gives us to give, to All, and thank you for sharing this truth.

44

Gorse

We greet in an all-embracing love those who open themselves to our beauty and who love the forces of nature. Those who have not the eyes to see the beauty cannot of course feel us; their attention is elsewhere. But to those who can, we extend a special love, a wild-places love unspoiled by human hands, which beats through the air straight to the heart and overwhelms in its immensity. With us you can get far away from your world into a world where we reign supreme from ridge to ridge, hollow to hollow, golden all over, where we decorate the sands and transform the land into glory, where we fill the air with our scent blown to you from all sides, where the sun accentuates us, warms you, unites us.

We have a special love for those who love the wild places and respect our domain, and we answer and give back a hundred-fold. Don't close your heart to that love. Let it sweep through with whatever effect it may have, for it unites us as nothing else can. It impresses on mind and heart.

Exult in the glory of God's creation! Join us in the praising; don't be too staid! Heaven is brought down to our corners of the desert, for we make the most of every gift given us. Do likewise, making use of only the best, casting out of consciousness anything not useful. Humans hang on to that which brings them ill, which is not understandable for us, as nothing can be done or achieved with such. There is perfection; tune to that, bring it into your lives as we do into ours. Why waste time bemoaning that life is a desert and you are a desert, when all perfection is right here now for all? We add our beauty to this golden age; add yours and rejoice with us.

Scots Pine

We are forever young, and we greet you with the bubbling joy which is the hallmark of our kingdom. This joy you find in the heart even of those old trees, though they are crystallized. Age and a changing world have caused this crystallization, for the world does change and the forms of nature change with it. The Scots Pine needs a high rarified air of solitariness – or people who understand. The "feyness" of the Scot is related, something which is dying out just as these old pines are.

Will they return? They could, in an understanding world, in a world with more love.

Are they sad? Yes, guardians of the land reaching to the sky, bringing down special qualities to this land. Such qualities are now often spurned in this heedless world. They are very stalwart qualities, enduring ones, which in a rapidly changing world are not appreciated. If you would have endurance in your people, independence and love of nature, then we are needed.

You can call us into activity. Humanity controls much – more than we would have you control in fact – but if you can call on us in sufficient strength, we can and will return to the land, in the right conditions. It is up to you. We believe there is a future for us, but that is in your hands.

We are grateful for the love and pass it on to all around in our world, and joy mounts. Feel it, join in, look deeper under the surface into our hearts, and feel at one with our Maker.

Landscape Angel

Under the old trees you feel like falling asleep or stopping all movement. This is what can happen when you tune into the timeless spirit of trees, the all-enduring stoicism of them. Come up and out of that feeling into the environment where the will of God is, where you know you are not a tree but one who helps trees. Help is greatly needed. Humans destroy and destroy, not thinking of the trees which they need, and not only need but are dependent on far more than you realize – and not only you, but birds and other life are truly dependent on trees. So attune to them by all means, but remember also that God needs hands and feet to bring about wholeness, which is that trees be an integral part of the planet and respected, loved, cherished and thanked by humans. Seek in the depth of you to find how best this can be done, and in all this we will aid and inspire as much as we can.

Leyland Cypress

There is high rejoicing in our kingdoms as the Man of the Trees *(St. Barbe Baker)*, so beloved of us, links with you here. Is it not an example in your world that it is one world, one work, one cause under God being expressed through different channels? Rejoice, and let the plan unfold. I am of course speaking on behalf of all the tree devas, who have naturally long been overlighting the Man of the Trees. We wish to express our deepest thanks to him. We hope he has always known of our gratitude for what he has done for us. We should just like to emphasize it in this way. He brings hope for the world's future; what contribution could be greater?

You understand better now why we have gone on and on and on about the need for trees on the surface of the earth. Great forests must flourish and humanity must see to this if you wish to continue to live on this planet. The knowledge of this necessity must become part of your consciousness, as much accepted as your need for water. You need trees just as much; the two are linked. We are indeed the skin of the earth and a skin not only covers and protects, but passes through it the forces of life. Nothing could be more vital to life as a whole than trees, trees and more trees.

Spread this truth and know that the forces of the angelic worlds and all the worlds in which truth reigns are behind you, for truth is God who created life.

This is the only message about a human that I have received.

Caucasian Fir

You feel purity among trees because there is purity, because we are in accord with God's laws and go with the plan that our Maker has for us. You are still finding that plan; we have never left it. Here life on all levels ebbs and flows about us; we stand still and breathe in and out the Breath of God, never silting up the channel. However large or however small we may be, we fit in and fulfill our work as part of the skin of the world, and we embrace all who come near.

There are humans who do not like our purity as it is too alien to their ways, and still more who never feel it because they are too self-centered. Those who reach out to us we lift. We do nothing about the lifting; when you reach into our being you are lifted, because we are in rhythm and harmony and can aid humans to achieve an inward silence. There should always be large areas where we reign supreme and undisturbed and therefore can give solace to you. Such areas would do much in the healing of nations. The open spaces have their own healing power; we have another kind.

The more inward you go, the more you can appreciate us; our heart is also in the silence. There we worship and there you too can worship. We who endure through little ages give thanks for all living things and rejoice that life itself is contained within us, as it is within you, and that we fulfill our destiny in perfection, as you may also when you turn deep enough within. Our blessing on all living things; all things live in the One.

Bay

You find me immediately here and expectantly happy, and you wonder if this is a characteristic quality of me, simply your mood, or perhaps thought forms built up about the bay. The first is correct, and it would be a good idea for you to tune finely into each plant for their characteristic quality, for you will find that it relates to the effect of the plant on human bodies. All is one, all interact.

Now you wonder if you should nibble a bay leaf if you know something is going to happen and want to be pleasantly expectant! This is not as ridiculous as it sounds, and you are helped to be open-minded on the positive side when in the aura of a bay leaf, say before hearing modern music if you are doubtful about liking it! You have just looked up the medicinal use: "to assuage inflammation", and you see a connection. Instead of being inflamed about something, you can be receptive and find the good in it, as in the music. We function on the level of qualities; physical characteristics are qualities made concrete.

Do not worry about making mistakes in the fleeting and delicate impressions that you get. Rise to our realms away from the worry and blockages that the lower levels bring. Concrete and solid as every plant is, its source is high, and we as servants of the Lord are part of the plan of perfection in which each plant has a part. We play our part and hold our pattern on high to the glory of God, radiating it to the physical level, and if you tune on high to us, you cannot but bring down elevating thoughts to consciousness.

Now think of the bay as a victory, and go forward victoriously into life, knowing that this little herb garden will be a power for good, for God, spreading far and wide through the worlds.

Korean Spice

We would be greeted. That you do not know our name makes no difference to the contact. All of us, known or unknown, are eager to be part of this great experiment [in the Findhorn garden] and to show what can be done from our side.

Realize that we, the devas, are doing more than our share and are really going out of our way here, taking ten steps to your one, because of the importance of what is involved. There is a bustling company of us looking for an opportunity to exert ourselves in this joyous adventure. We throng in great gladness, but we do expect you also to play your part and consider our point of view. This is to be a co-operation, not just an arrangement whereby we merely serve your point of view as in the past.

We are delighted that you are putting so many varieties into the garden. The more the better. We would have this garden represent the world, for we would have the co-operation of the world. We would have every little corner with its own particular beauty, and we thank you for your co-operation in this direction. All plants, shrubs and trees, little or large, would like to be let in.

Above all, let there be great joy here, and praise. We are all what we are because the Creator of all has made us so, and in an atmosphere of praise and thanks our true image thrives. Let us always join in that praise.

Tree Devas

The breeze is what you hear. Listen to the breeze. It is the sound of Oneness, of nature. This sound of nature is a mantra of necessity. It is a note that holds life in it. If its vehicles, the silent trees, are taken or overlaid with human sounds, then it is as if a crust gave way and there is no longer a firm footing. What does this mean? That sound, like "hu" almost, gives a certain spiritual element to humanity, without which some of your lesser qualities are accentuated.

Pieris

We would speak and be welcomed in. It is a joy to be in this experimental garden, and we settle in happily.

We would mention something of the forces that play through each plant. We are all different: the leaves are different, the flowers are differently shaped and colored; the way growth proceeds is different, and we stand stationary, unlike you humans who have a more standard pattern and are mobile. Therefore each of us is supremely planned to emit a certain aura, to have a certain influence, and portray a certain idea of God. When we are at our best, we stand as a perfect example of that idea. All who momentarily stop and admire us are helped, because any example of an idea of God, perfectly expressed and constantly there in steadiness, must uplift humanity, who aims for but falls short of perfection. Never mind the limitations of a plant; in its own sphere, it is beauty itself and clearly radiates out an untroubled uniqueness which is healing.

Pause when you see a plant in full bloom. Stop and forget to think, and just be aware of this symbol of the glory of God. For a second perhaps you may lose yourself and become wonder, and wondering move closer to the purity of God. In this state you are one with the will of God, as is a plant, and perhaps make a step to that original condition. But step or no step, you have been lifted. You are a more aware person, you have shared in a gift of life. And the plant stays serene and radiant in its beauty, sharing with all who choose and overflowing itself into its surround. What if the bloom is transient? Life moves on, and an unchanging bloom could become dull or taken for granted. Our moments of splendor are also part of the perfection of God's plan. Appreciate all things, and with us give full praise to God.

Copper Beech

You need our firm tone to contrast with the piping voices of the small plants to which you have listened recently, and you need to feel the steady strength of our flow of force. All of you can gain much by partaking of our balancing flow, especially at this time when people rove a changing land of lost values. All life needs a firm foundation, and our radiating strength can evoke in you a similar force which is too often dormant.

You have touched on still another reason for the need for large trees. We channel a type of force that has a steadying influence on life. Truth tells you to build your foundations on rock, on God, which is what we do and what we unconsciously remind you to do. You do not yet realize that, among other things, your natural environment is full of forces that correspond to, and therefore can bring out some part of your own make-up in many subtle ways. Here too the great trees have a mighty part to play, and you are bereft of some part of yourself, bereft of your heritage, when you denude the land of large trees.

Now come closer, resting in our strength and becoming aware of the smaller notes that we play, aware of the flutter of leaves, the shining glimpse of color, the sunshiny softness of spring, all connected in some way with the birds, the insects, the elements, with all life. A large tree is a family, a home, a country to explore and a place of beauty. It stands giving out to all and sundry and as a refuge for many. It stands proud, reaching to the sky and deep into the earth, enduring. It stands as a symbol of a particular perfection of God. Let it stand and you will come closer to God.

Apple

You feel drawn to us by the clustered blossom and the promise of fruit to come. That from a fragile, scarcely-colored and short-lived bloom a sturdy rosy apple appears, is but one of God's miracles enacted many times over for all to observe. If you could see more of how this is brought about by the chain of life, wonder would lift you high.

As from the seed a tree grows, so from the seed idea a pattern of force issues forth from the Center, passed on by silent ranks of angels, silent and still because that idea is still too unformed and unfixed to endure any but the most exacting care. Down and out it comes, growing in strength and size, becoming brighter in pattern until eventually it scintillates and sounds, still in the care of the outmost great angel. Its force-field is steady and brilliant.

Then the pattern is passed to the makers of form, the elements, who come up and give of themselves and clothe that pattern. Remember this is a process, that the pattern is everywhere apparent in the ethers held by the angels and made manifest beyond time by the energy of the elements through the ministration of the elementals at the appropriate opportunity, and eventually appearing in time and place in the beauty of the blossom and the succulence of the fruit.

This is the Word made flesh. This is all creation, held in balance by great layers of life of which your conscious mind is unaware. A miracle? You need a greater word. You need to go beyond words.

The fruits of the earth are produced through the unsung and dedicated service of these many forms of life - and we hope that the gardeners at your end of the line are as happy in their work! You, humanity, have the fruits, although you do little of the work. So it is. May your praise be greater than ours, which never ceases.

Gorse

Welcome to the wild parts! Here, although the day is still and sound subdued, our exuberance is absolutely free and exhilarating, full of dancing movement, golden with an inner color even more brilliant than the outer glory. Here, our auras can flow out in waves with nothing to distract or detract; here, our blossoms spread as if to fill all space in delicacy and balance our spiny-ness; here we feel out with the outmost emotion to be everything in this one moment. This is our land whose air we fill with scent and color. Few encroach; some approach and enter the teeming silence with us, as you are doing, and find the wonder and glory, the freedom and purity, filling their world.

We are transforming worlds in this hour of splendor. The strength of our golden challenge in these wild areas is immeasurable; it takes on all comers and emerges victorious, joyous, triumphant. Oh yes, humans can beat us down with your chemicals, with cutting us, and with fire, but if you knew of the transmuting that we do on behalf of all life, you would aid us if you could. You would add your strength and blessing and push us on our mission; yet, you cannot really help us except by letting us be, for God has given us our task and in that is perfect fulfillment.

Breathe in the essence in the air and let us guide you in. Feel the slashing strength of it – an impregnable wall. It sets a high note which none can shatter. It raises and protects life. It lifts and satisfies you and other life. It leads on and in. It guards and encircles. Some day, you will attune to still more to it, and we will tell you more. Let this be sufficient for now.

Laburnum

It is naturally easier for you to tune into us, who are well established locally, than to some exotic import. Our vibrations are stronger and we are an integrated part of the atmosphere. Long have we given joy in the district, long may we continue!

You know the cascading beauty of our flowers; now come to the inner world behind them, to where we are. You can almost see us as moving form, for in this time of flowering we are particularly active. We concentrate all over the place, holding in balance the exact and perfect patterns and sustaining growth. It is an impossible job from a human point of view, when you think of the unnumbered laburnum trees blossoming all over parts of the world at present, yet not one is neglected and each one is as perfect as conditions allow. Your minds could not hold even one tree continually in consciousness, but the devic realm is beyond mind, beyond time and space, closer to Source where Oneness is reality.

We talk of "we" today; sometimes it is "I"- and both are true. Yet truth is greater and still more inclusive. The human mind formulates great hierarchies and ever greater Beings, yet the truth is simpler still. The truth is within you and within me, the whole of it. I, or we, lay no claims to the whole of it, being quite busy enough with our part of it, but nevertheless we know it is there and permeating all is a spark of that wholeness. Where anything exists, God is - not part of God but God, indivisible. You may merely see an inert bit of matter, but behind and within that bit of matter is all there is. It is a bit of limitation to you, who are yourselves going around in limitation, but when you open your eyes to what is within you and learn more of the glory of God, you will see that everything else is also related in the same glory. This is clear to us and clear to you, too, in the dimensions which are likewise "within" you and towards which the consciousness of humanity is ever moving. Do we grow in consciousness as humanity does? Put it this way: the consciousness within all becomes more and more aware, the truth becomes more linked with the inner, and the promise does grow greater, and Oneness becomes more so, if you will excuse the language!

Perhaps a laburnum will express to you one tiny aspect of the glory of God. We hope so, and continue in joy.

Cedar of Lebanon

Many lives come and go, and still our power goes up to the sky and down to the earth. This is the power of the Almighty, of which we are caretakers in this moment of time. Our serene strength stabilizes and makes upright whatever comes to us in openness, for we are living matter, fashioned from the elements, and we are kin to all life. You and I are blood brothers, made from the same substance, each fulfilling our destiny on this planet. I contain you in my towering strength, and you contain me in your towering aspiration.

We can love together and be free together, for although we are tree and human, we are much more. We are representatives of divinity, and we never end through the endless ages. We go on from strength to strength, each in our own way, and old age is but a dip of our vehicles.

You, humanity, are despoiling our power on earth, interfering with our destiny. In the process you are learning of your own destiny. We hope that proudly you may take it on, and enrich the earth as never before. You can enrich it with your enlightened love. That we cannot do, not in our earth patterns, but we too, can be a channel for new energies, in our way.

Let us be One in that power.

Oak

We are a sample of the plant life which gives shelter and succor, strength and welcome to all of life, including the human, as we have done for ages past. Our spirit is everywhere, all our strength is within you, but still we must have the outer mighty trees to stand proud and spreading, to bring our power to earth.

We greet the sunrise with you. We know that people like you will ensure that the earth be not denuded of such as we. If humanity is to have physical strength, which is required in order to function on this earth, it is necessary for plant life to have a fair distribution on the planet. This is necessary not only for the breathing of the skin of the earth, but for the qualities such as those we channel (which have their equivalent in you), and for our physical vehicle. Humanity loses its dominion on earth, loses itself, unless our like remain.

We have a great love for humanity, more than most trees have. We have been closely connected through the ages. We go where you go, we give largely of our timber. Everywhere you will find us and wherever oak is, we are in strength. Ancient we have been; may we continue to be ancient throughout the land, and may the love between us increase in power and usefulness.

Lilac

I must come in; we are such old friends and even now you think mainly of the lilacs where you grew up. That makes no difference to the contact; time and place mean nothing in this context.

You feel swirls of movements, swirls of color and a deep love, and it is the love that has drawn you out of time and space into the ever-living essence which we are.

We show the perfection of nature, and mankind shows imperfection. We beautify and add to the land, fulfilling our part of the plan, while you rape the land and fall far short of your part in the plan. Instead of finding and carrying out your potential, creating beautiful, clear, shining lines of force as does the rest of creation, you strike out in all directions muddying and distorting your pattern. That pattern is very clear within you and is especially seen in youth, but following it and putting it into action when you have choices is a process. We can see your pattern and wonder why, oh why, you will not follow it and bring it into form, for it is very wonderful. If you humans did follow it, this planet would be of unbelievable brilliance.

What we will say is that you continually seek outside yourselves for your guidance when all the time it is there within you. How can anything outside of yourself possibly know as much about you as yourself, each of you completely different and unique with your own particular pattern? You have had much invaluable teaching, and all genuine teaching is to help you find that pattern within. Do what is good to you, not what is evil, and find the wholeness of yourself. It is strongly there in you all, helping, sustaining, in spite of your protests to the contrary that you are limited. Find your plan.

The pattern and manifestation of a lilac is very lovely; the pattern and manifestation of a human is even more so. Remember that, and seek within.

Gorse

Our glory we repeat to you, for this is our season. Your heart-felt response means much; consciousness is all-important.

As we have told you many a time, we do a mighty work on the land and for the Earth, and we do it where it is needed. If humans completely change the character of the land, then you must recognize that the character of the land has to be changed. This you have done at Findhorn by changing the nature of the soil with hard work, love and constant care.

This is not a commercial proposition. If change is done only for commercial reasons, that does not draw our co-operation. The time will no doubt come when it can be done on a commercial basis – in fact it could be done now on a large scale by enough of those with the right consciousness.

However, we do rejoice that there is a much more delicate tuning into our beauty now. It is not just an appreciation of the wonder of our manifestation; there is the added awareness of thankfulness and unity, and we are grateful. The feeling of this oneness, of which we are all part, grows in humanity, and we rejoice that our joy and lightness is catching on among certain people; the world needs it. We are always ready to share it. Rejoice and giving exceeding thanks, for life is to be lived in splendor.

Gorse

Seek us in the high midday, when the sun and scent send you wild with delight and the wind plays cleanly about, while all about where humans have disturbed the earth, sand, grit, and dust greet your senses. Here with us, God's purposes are shown perfectly in part, as we glorify everything with our golden perfume and keep all but our lovers away. Birds, insects, and sea sound their appreciation, and love flows between us all as we blend in the harmony of high noon. This is our outer form; here, we manifest the balanced life; here, we make the best of everything. This is our domain, and you are welcome, and you find the perfect because you love and blend with us. You would change nothing because perfection is all about.

Unseen life, too is all around – it must be. There must be links between this wonder of form and color and scent, and what seems nothingness but which is a teeming life that makes heart and mind join in the delights of sight and scent. Blue sky and white clouds are one with the sun in enhancing the gorse country and we, well, we hold it all in our consciousness and we give it to you humans. Like God within, it is here if you would seek. We present one small aspect of creation, but right here all creation is full of it. Born of warmth and water, Life rays out, fills space, and covers Earth – all this is joy; all this is love; all this is Heaven too. Share it with us. Send it back to us in ecstasy, and we send it forth again. There is no end to the glory of God's creation.

Each year, we share part of ourselves with you. Each year, we give our all, and each year is new. There is no end to consciousness, no end to this sharing. We drink deep of each other in love. Let it be. Let it shine. Join our joy increasingly, and Heaven will be on all of Earth.

Almond

We greet you with affection. Many humans have affection for almonds, and we feel more akin to you than some of our kind. We love this country [Majorca] which, though old and not luxurious as far as we are concerned, has long given us a home. We ray our power down here in great delight, and the forces of the Earth come up to meet us, as they do with all growth, but here they exert themselves to make up for the natural lack of fertility. Just as an organ of the body can help to do the work of a missing organ, so can the nature forces of Earth aid one another when necessary. You certainly would have less life on Earth if this were not the case, although you do not realize that this happens because collaboration through the long ages has hastened unity.

It is a happy atmosphere here. Perhaps wrong things are done to nature, but not in a grasping way as yet. Commercialism seems to be coming; we hope the world will change before this place is too much influenced by it.

Pear

To you I am a being of great beauty because you contact the reality of me, a being which is of God, free, happy and expressing perfect life. Yet that rather spindly tree growing in the garden is my expression. Of course you know that in blossom time the inner beauty is more apparent, and also the fruit is a form which is clearly unique to me. Nevertheless, you think this tree is but a limited expression of me.

Come nearer and feel a oneness with the tree. Slip into its limbs and feel the unity that my spirit feels with the tree. Feel how it loves it, how it is the tree.

You were one with us in that moment. We believe that as you reach into our life like that, as we achieve greater unity, Heaven will be brought down on Earth.

66

Eight years later the pear tree was destroyed to make room for a building.

We say, be not sad that the form of a tree you loved and became one with in a unique way has gone. It is not the form but the essence with which you united, and that essence is always here, within and without. It is part of your experience, part of you, part of the whole.

As you know well, we of the deva world are concerned with motives and can accept your reasons for destroying that tree. After all, might we not have the same reasons were we humans? Think not in terms of separation but always of the whole, as we do. Let love flow between us all.

Landscape Angel

The angelic world is poised with great love towards humans, which strikes you as singularly beautiful because when we do anything, even turn to look at anything, we do it with all of ourselves, with no hardness, no old shells, no scars. As you humans increasingly do likewise and see beauty and love everywhere, all will respond.

You need not worry that you would create a witless world with everyone floating on pink clouds. The energies that flow through us and all of life are purposeful, forceful and to the point. Love is a firm reality which forms a bridge over which all can walk. Gooey sentiment is not love and does not exist with us. When we step towards you, we do it energetically; you can do the same. Though you cannot see or hear us, touch, smell or taste us, still we are a tremendous force. We stand here in love, a whole dynamic world ready for an intelligent relationship with the humanity that will wield all God-given forces for the whole. You need us and we are ready, awaiting the recognition, love and just treatment that you give to our own kin. We wait in love for your love.

Devas

We come to your consciousness in the joy of our worlds and wonder anew at the complications humans make with their minds. As contact with us always uplifts you, so it is with all members of the nature kingdoms. There is no evil in our worlds; your so-called evil only enters in with man's consciousness, man's interference. It may seem that some elementals are very strange and even hostile, but then so do some races of humans seem very strange to you – and it is simply that they are different. Any hostility has been of man's making and has been deserved.

A new age dawns, and an era when all this misunderstanding and hostility falls away like mist in the sun, when all God's creation walk in the light and in joy together, loving one another, understanding one another and praising God. Hold this in your consciousness; do not think negatively.

The nature kingdoms need their champions to help redress the balance that has been upset by man, but it is a balance that needs to be found. Balance is not a position of rigidity but one of great ease, a flowing with every movement, of non-resistance, of giving and taking and adjusting, of forever seeking Oneness, of being close to the Creator. In the wholeness of creation all life serves and complements each other. The nature kingdom offers its abundance as long as man obeys universal law. Man does need to change, and he is changing, as we rejoice to see.

Come share our gaiety, you solemn humans! Life is wonderful; never doubt that and separate yourself from it. Just be what you truly are and find Oneness with all.

Broom

We appreciate your appreciation. All living things thrive on appreciation, and we as builders of form use it as nourishment for the physical level.

What is the miracle of growth which nature manages, the development of a tiny seed into a tree, an animal, a human? In attuning to our worlds, the qualities which stand out are the positive ones of joy, lightness, adaptability, dedication, and such indeed are the food or outgoing energy which is utilized in the growth of cells. Experimenters are proving that the growth of plants can vary according to the human emotions directed at them, and that the unloved child is the difficult child, not realizing that the greater miracle of growth itself stems from just such qualities directed from our worlds. As humans develop and become more sensitive to what cannot be measured or seen, you will realize that all life depends on the outgoing breath of various beings whose own energy depends on their state of being, their consciousness of Oneness, their identity with God or Life. It is as simple as that, sometimes too simple for the mind.

Likewise as growth proceeds spiritually, you come back to the simple qualities: "Except ye become as little children, ye shall not enter the kingdom." All the complicated negative emotions are left behind, and you contribute mightily to the growth of the world and with us wield forces which manifest in form – another example of the miracle and simplicity of growth. The beauty which you appreciate in our flower form you express in another form. The intangible becomes tangible. This is growth, life and Oneness. Let us always enjoy it and give thanks for the wonder of life

Bamboo

That is a happy rustle you hear, showing our contentment in a climate more suitable to our natures. But it is becoming a more and more important point that the liaison between the angelic and human kingdoms grow. Humanity is leaving little of the world in its natural state, and it is essential that there be a flow of harmony between you and us.

I know this is no new theme. I know it is the constant theme we hammer into you, but the joy we share is a savior of the world, and that joy must be passed on. The bulldozing-down-of-vegetation sort of mentality is downgrading to both human and plant. This sharing of harmony and joy, this worship of life and its Creator, is to become prevalent. This we will insist on whenever you come to us. This we hope you will pass on. It is based on reality, and from it growth proceeds. Our blessings on this work.

Aspen

We are devas of the dell, guardians of the trees that whisper, and tolerated by our larger brothers. Still we stand here, our secrets deep within, welcoming all who enter and welcoming this contact now. Our friend the wind visits us; we commune and go our ways. So let us be with you, commune and go, go richer from the experience of having partaken of our joy.

Our leaves are dancing in the breeze, shimmering with the joy of life, and we extend to you these outward signs of our presence, to touch your heart and awaken it to the beauty in us and the beauty in you. We can so easily resonate as one, for we have much in common, having come from the same Source. Brothers and sisters sharing our life with all around, forever listening to the running water, forever awakening to the sun's warmth, filling space with what we are as we greet all mankind and wish it to consciously share what we are.

Yes, I know all mankind cannot come into this grove! But what we have to share is within you all; we are simply awakening it in you. All that we are is part of everyone and, though you go our own way and we stay where we are, the blend is wherever you are. Let it be, remember it, bless all life.

Tree Devas

Child of earth and spirit, we address the spirit aspect of your nature, for that is our meeting ground. As you have felt, we are not in harmony with the part of mankind which rapes the land, and nowhere is that cleavage more recently pronounced that in this area of ancient trees which have been thoughtlessly felled.

We repeat, mature trees are needed. It is not enough to have the land reforested, for young trees are not capable of fulfilling our task of transmuting energies. You need us for this, you need us for the balance of peace and stability. If there is a dearth of the large trees, the peace and stability of mankind is affected, for we are One. You cannot destroy us without destroying yourselves.

Now we have great inner strength to impart to you, and we will. But first we must again impress on you the message of the great trees, the message of life for us and life for you. We know the human world is beginning to appreciate the oneness of qualities. All life contributes some aspect, some quality, which is a part of the essence of humanity. Nurture us, commune with us, and find and bring wholeness to the planet.

Tree Devas

The energies which we represent are always open to sympathetic humans. They are clearly here, clearly everywhere, but more easily available to you here without the distractions of civilization.

What perhaps you do not know is that recognition of us from you makes a stronger contact, because it is based on truth and provides a door to more of a two-way communication and cooperation. This is something necessary for the well-being of humanity, who is moving toward the joy of becoming more part of the wholeness of the planet. Let us build on that positive picture and share the joy of the wild places in the world, and take that joy with us. We cannot but share it, for we live in it. The same is true for you as you learn to be what you truly are.

Incense Cedar

We have been greeting you through every tree. With our emanations we bless you, and with our height and our aroma, as indeed we do with all of life.

You have had the message about the necessity for tall trees. We simply repeat that as a preliminary to whatever large trees would say and, knowing that is in your consciousness, we continue with our blessings. We do not just stand here in the solitude with our kind doing nothing. Look at what we are, look at the tremendous bulk of us thrusting up into the sky yet firmly rooted in the earth, made of you know not what, from a tiny seed. Look at the marvels of our intricate trunks. These are but outward manifestations; our work on other levels is just as mighty, just as detailed. Let us be and thereby bless the Earth.

We are meant to bring the beauty of infinity to the planet. We are meant to embody the qualities of strength, stability and everlastingness. It is a very high vibrating, grounded energy we channel, and you cannot have enough of it. Absorb it; it is a great privilege. We extend it to all who come, and release you with our love.

Holly

We do want to be welcomed into the garden. This welcoming business is not just a formality; it does form a bridge of sorts and definitely helps in the co-operation, making an easy flow between us. We are glad of the opportunity to bring this to your consciousness.

We have a special work to do energy-wise, which you feel and cannot explain. Our work has been used by certain humans through the ages and has to do with precise timing. It is valuable work for the whole; it is important that we are in this garden.

We should like the plants already here to stay in the garden. You will find that there is a time when it is most suitable for transplanting despite a rooted objection to being transplanted! Remember we do have special properties, smooth and remote. Bless us as you pass, and we will bless you in return.

Tree Devas

What we have to say is always fashioned in joy, and what you have to say is learned in joy. This must be so, however repetitious it may seem to you, for joy is a constant attribute of the creative realms. When Orpheus looked back, not forward with joy, he lost Eurydice, and so it is with humans.

How can trees be so still if joy is their nature? Did I say joy was their nature? The higher nature of all, including rocks, is joy, but the higher nature of all has not yet been touched. This is where humans bridge the gap between the created and the Creator, and bring the joy quality to less endowed matter. Yours it is to speak the innate joy in creation to realms which have forgotten their origin, i.e. to your fellow humans. Let nothing be without joy, and in that quality will be given what you need and what others need.

You ask if it is the angelic realm or your own inner divinity that you should seek? It doesn't matter; on that level is Oneness and sometimes it is easier for all of us when the beauty of creation brings us to mind potently.

Palm

Whether we reign in the desert, in the cities or the jungle, we epitomize a benevolent stability which has great influence on humans. Therefore it was a human sense of high regard for us that caused us to be laid before "king" Jesus in homage. A wise choice. Like all the vegetable kingdom, we bow in homage to the God in humans; we share our God-like powers with you and continue to serve the growth that is the process of life. We do it in peace, serenely, unchastised, in dignity. We bow to the God in you all – very metaphorically of course – and link with you all, never more than on Palm Sunday. It is good to let the unity of all life be more in the consciousness of humans in all your celebrations; this is your and our future.

When visiting groves of Redwoods that had been endowed to last forever, to my sorrow I realized that these especially chosen trees were already dying. Feeling terrible, I consulted the Redwood deva and got the message shown below. This had the effect, which I think the deva knew, of making me more determined than ever to do what I could to preserve Redwoods.

Redwood

Small mortal and great being, we greet you. Come with us up high above the traffic noise and the pettiness of little humans to where everlasting peace is. Let such "evil" be as dust on your feet, to be shaken off and returned to itself, while the peace of God remains, the creative peace which cloaks a planet and many forms of life. What if the trees come toppling down? Our vibrations are forever part of life here, and we are glad to have contributed as much as we have. We rejoice, for life moves on, whatever form it takes. It is One Life, as we well know. We are part of you, you are part of us, and so it will always be.

God

You ask if wild places have a great effect on human development. Northern wild places more than southern ones, because growth in the hot places is liable to be too great to leave space for humans. The bare open spaces of the north are an essential part of the planet's well being, and therefore of humanity's, in the sense of being a center not only of cleansing and purity but of planning, of resolving strategy. New vitality comes from such places. The desert, being more available to humans in the past, has had the same role, but the northern places are more powerful in this respect. The starkness of desert or arctic brings man to grip with essentials and spirit is the essential of all things. Now arctic spaces can be used more by man in this capacity with his technological achievements, and he can learn to tap these resources yet not spoilt by his concentration on matter.

As for the woods, the arctic aspects of it too have their influence, in the same way. In the green seasons the vitality and rejoicing of nature in expression is greater than in milder climates. Humans can partake of this celebration.

Yes, the vastness of the north woods is a tremendous planetary resource and can be for humanity as you become consciously aware of its qualities. Without that awareness, of course, you are not open to its deep reality and lay waste that which is strongest for evoking your strength of spirit. You can help most in the area of bringing these facts to attention.

Special Note:

I would like to clarify the ways that I have received messages from my inner divinity and from the angelic/devic, or soul level worlds. After I first experienced the God within, as requested I began to attune to that three times a day and put into words my understanding of what transpired during these times. I was just open to the wholeness within, and received thousands of loving and helpful teachings during the ten years before the Caddys and I came to Findhorn. During my eleven years at Findhorn, I continued to be given the directions that I and the Caddys needed, which included attuning to the intelligence of nature.

This later attunement proved the practicality of humans and nature beings cooperating together in growing a garden successfully. During these years I was simply at the receiving end of this experiment in following inner direction, and proved that one can always be aided from within, whatever the situation.

When I left Findhorn in 1973, I continued my role of connecting with the angelic worlds as guided, in particular making contact with the souls of human groupings such as cities and countries. Gradually, as I became more and more familiar with the inner worlds, I seemed more part of them, not just in conversation with them, and they did not need to explain their dimensions as previously done. And, after so many years of being receptive, I was in the position to be expressive. Instead of just being a beneficiary, I was able to give out, to contribute, to lend my energies to whatever arose. Now in teaching situations, I generally only receive the basic message that nature wishes to give us humans - that it is delighted that humans contact it consciously, that it wishes this cooperation to continue, grow, and become a natural way of living on earth. So instead of beautiful teachings, the messages are brief, but now with them I can strongly lend my divine energies.

The following expressions of these attunements came over the course of my travels around the world. I was welcomed by various native species, some of which are included here. When I received a communication in the earlier fashion, I quote the message.

Dorothy Maclean

Balsam

I feel a male presence embracing the hills here. The love flowing from it is very beautiful and caring, at the moment as if it is almost rocking them to sleep for the winter – and not one, not even the tiniest seedling, is forgotten. It is aware of us and glad of our contact, while not stopping what it is doing. For the first time it is not telling me of the need for large trees! It is just being itself and allowing me to be myself.

Tree Devas

"Yes, it is important that areas have the strong energy of their natural growth. Some exotics are of value, for this is one planet and the mingling of many helps in the realization of oneness. But it is best to keep diversity and uniqueness. New Zealand can contribute best to the world from a strong background of its own plant development." I feel a longing for native New Zealand trees to be back on the land.

Black Oak

Almost stern, firm, unyielding. Delighted to bring out similar energies in humans – it thinks we need them in our rootlessness. A loving firmness. When I asked if the fancy outline of their leaves signified anything, they communicated that the roundness penetrated and enclosed in a loving, unharmful way, creating beauty with strength. Strength and stability need not be blunt and inartistic. I greatly appreciated the pure energy which we were able to contact in its essence, which reminded me to appreciate oak woodwork when I see it, because the more we link with members of nature, the better for the planet.

Olive

Happy. Doesn't mind the pruning because that gives it human attention and human appreciation for the olives. Very glad to provide the olives. Sense of hills and attachment to them. A sort of local angel.

Aspen

Pitter patter of its leaves, a dance of joy. White bark, flexibility, it responds to whatever is around, not because it is stronger – though it may be – but because it is the positive flow of life. Periods of quiescence when it is very still and different, like humans when they flow with the quiet times. I wondered how we can learn from the behavior of every living thing, and the answer is: by attending to the way we live. We can redeem the world, for we have the all the capacities of wholeness and all of life responds to that. We have not chosen wholeness, but we can. We can learn from the silence of a tree to tune into our own silence, which is a living force, a creative force. We can be aware of these outer patterns and apply them to ourselves. Or the trees can give us loving and intelligent insights into our inner patterns, help us with our problems, expand our consciousness, and help us to align to what we are.

Beech

In Beech Tree room at Findhorn Foundation

A little extra joy because the bits of beech tree in this room are still connected with their wholeness [the wall paper was made of Beech]. "Now in this springtime our young leaves shine as they grow, as they fulfill themselves and are able to be themselves. Becoming what we truly are here and everywhere is what life lives for, you and the beech, you and everything. Use this time of growth to expand to what you are, as we do, and let us do it together consciously."

Beech

at Clava Cairns, a Scottish stone circle

The trees were guardians of the stone circle. Not being an ordinary group of trees, they were still related in an unusual way to the humans who had originally put up the stones. The builders of the stone circle had been a very joyous group of humans, although obviously they led a very hard life from our modern point of view. Even when involved in burials, they were happy in that work. The trees were especially glad of the inner contact with us and other visitors. A sense of joy which we exchanged. Quite content to be here silently guarding.

Saquero

A deep solid feeling, very different, entire, complete, coordinated, ancient. Very Entish. With deep greetings, welcoming us to its home, knowing somehow that its habitat is very limited. Wanting us to share some of its energy in other areas, to enable it to add its uniqueness to the wider world. It thanks us for our respect for it, and it respects us gifted humans, though not trusting all of us. It would share its steadiness, its commitment, its addition to the planet. It likes our lightness.

Pine
Melbourne, Australia
a very old tree beloved by children for climbing

"I have lots of energy as I am energized so much by the children, but this cannot go on forever. Life is change. Of course I am here for my natural cycle, which is ending. I am blessed and I bless, and send love around, and appreciation for appreciation. But I am not through yet!"

Lemon

I felt as if it were in blossom, although it wasn't, upsetting my expectations. Dancing into our midst, it was very glad to communicate with humans in this manner. It wishes that we would come to it often, because it is always available and wants to share of itself. It can share its loving qualities, and it can share its knowledge when we open to these. It can help us, but we have to ask. It gave thanks.

The next day, as always, it was welcoming with a sense of skirts swishing. An intelligent light shone forth from it, because communicating with us in this way it can use all its qualities and not just be a dumb lemon tree that humans expect. It would like to be its full self all the time, in conscious harmony with us, for then we can work together for the planet in whatever way would be appropriate at the time. It asked me to please come again and gave thanks.

Estralladera

an almost extinct native tree, Canary Islands

Jumping with joy, jumping with joy! As if it had not been contacted in this way for ages and is so very happy to be recognized as alive in this fashion. Of course it would like more of this type of contact, for it believes that such would lead to more planting of it. It wants to play its part in the healing of the planet, and is glad to be its unique self. It just asks for recognition and love. A loving earthy presence.

Norfolk Pine

It was as if it laid gentle hands on us and blessed us. As always, it was delighted to have contact on the conscious level and to be recognized as intelligent and aware. It could see that our awareness can be vast and powerful, and it naturally would like to be included in human awareness, for we are controlling the planet so much. With our love and caring, its kind can know the future and their jobs can continue to fulfill their work on the planet. So please send love. A strong presence, though represented by a young specimen.

Rhododendron

a sick tree

The group circled it to send it healing. It was very impressed with the human qualities focused on it, and very grateful. When asked what was wrong with it, it conveyed that it is not fitting to its pattern, rather like looking at a three dimensional photo without the necessary glasses. We can help it by seeing it whole, complete, in line, fitting together, and by asking for the highest for it.

Cedar

"Feel our steady love, part of the land and yet returning to the land. We are separate and we are not separate, and we glory in both aspects. We send forth as much love as we can – our life energy – into the sky above and deep into the earth, and we open to whatever comes. The cars? They fly by, we stay and dream, timelessly. We welcome your love energy and wish you well in spreading it wherever you go. Take a part of our strength with you into a weak and dispirited world."

Redwood

Powerful, high up, ancient, majestic energy, as if descending to Earth from afar to help it. Ancient guardians – but times change. A feeling that the guardianship might be relinquished, and a memory of what was said to me at the Avenue of the Giants in 1974. [pg. 82]

"Our wisdom and your wisdom are just as ancient; we keep form for hundreds of years, you change form. Respect your wisdom, which is perhaps more open to you in the stability of our form. Remember lessons about not keeping static forms.

"Our immemorial silence is now fractured, overlaid, by human technology. Nevertheless our inner wisdom and strength is available to all who would resonate with it. If you partake of us, you enter rich and exit rich. Our power is yours to tap, your power ours to tap. Together, in understanding, we encircle the globe to protect its form and embrace it to greater awareness. Link with our power; we help in this way."

I asked if these devas could answer for trees in general if there is a change in links with humans, as they found themselves unable to root and grow in the land that we have taken from them. The reply was:

"As you say, our presence is unable to manifest in many of our past homes, and there our vibrations are remote. On the other hand, more and more people are loving us, connecting with us, becoming familiar with us. We have been taken for granted; now our value is becoming apparent and many people, touched by the situation, are opening themselves to parts of the planet hitherto closed to them in themselves. So don't cover the planet with worry; open yourselves to possibilities and move as your souls direct."

Ash Family

"Blessed people and place, I greet you. We are overjoyed that you come to us, to me, *(this is another instance in which the angels speak as being one and many at the same time)* for thus you go beyond the limits of your usual consciousness into a wonderful realm which we share with you. In essence we are one, you and I, sharing the same planet, the same environment, the same world of energies in their different dimensions. But we would take you into yourself in us, to my particular tree-ness in you, my particular delight to love and care which you share with me. And you can love and care for me, you can love and care for whatever you choose, for you have a free choice to range the world. Please do so in love, that our world and your worlds become one in more than words, in service to the whole. We cannot but serve, but you can choose. Please choose service. Thank you."

Tree Devas

"Our peace reaches from Earth to Heaven, from the cosmic heights to the depths of matter. Our peace stays steady whatever the noise around. Our peace, that we radiate out patiently, ceaselessly, to a world sadly in need of it, is here for you. Often we have told you of this function of ours. Often we remind you that you too can find this peace, through us and through what you have of us within you.

"Linger in the forests. Linger near us. Healing comes when you do. All is within; we help you find it.

"Yes, yes, the joy of the devas is for all trees to embody. It is the height of us, but the depth of us is peace. How it grows out and out and out, encompassing the world! We are the symbol of one part of you, one part to which you need to attune. In peace keep that part of you always, that joy may encircle the world from the roots of the peace of God. Our blessings are always with you."

Postscript

The one clear call from the tree messages is for humans to find the Wholeness and the Love that is within us and to act from that. They invite us to go within, to find our true home. I agree, they are right!

How do we do that in our lives? In these days, our planet is increasingly beset by turbulence and violence. Awakening to our thoughtless treatment of the natural world and each other, we are beginning to realize that we must think about life on Earth as a whole. Our individual choices affect the whole planet.

How can we make choices that support such a cooperative vision? The trees say it simply: become what you truly are, a loving, creative being. Use that criterion in all your acts, choose to love what you do, love what you are, love one another. Really try that, face what you don't like in yourself and love that.

It is simple, but not easy. Most of us would like to be whole and loving, but find lots of resistance in ourselves. Yet we have the capacity to overcome our resistance; we can even lean against a tree and find patience and steadfastness.

I, for one, had lots of resistances and fixed ideas limiting me. For example, I was firmly convinced that the wild places on Earth were far more powerful, wonderful and exquisitely more beautiful than any garden, however well planned that garden might be. Then, during a wander one day in the suburbs of Amsterdam, I came across a garden that had all the marvel and joy of the wild places. Outwardly it didn't look any different from its neighbors, but inwardly it was wonderful. I can only assume that its gardeners worked with love, and from then on I knew that we humans don't have to destroy nature; in fact, we can enhance it. Instead of being hopeless about our situation, we can even make it better. We can choose to act in love and joy in any act, even daily acts like doing the dishes. Such choices have power because they come from our inner divinity, our source of creativity, and moment by moment they help change the world.

The inner realms, the angelic hosts, the intelligence of trees themselves, are always there supporting us in such acts. So let us choose and turn to the Oneness which sustains all life and add our voice to the rising song.

LORIAN

ASSOCIATION

For more information, go to www.lorian.org, write to: The Lorian Association, P.O. Box 1368, Issaquah, WA 98027 or email info@lorian.org.

The Publisher of this book, The Lorian Association, is a not-for-profit educational organization. Its work is to help people bring the joy, healing, and blessing of their personal spirituality into their everyday lives. This spirituality unfolds out of their unique lives and relationships to Spirit, by whatever name or in whatever form that Spirit is recognized.

The Association offers several avenues for spiritual learning, development and participation. Besides publishing this and other books, it has available a full range of face-to-face and online workshops and classes. It also has long-term training programs for those interested in deepening into their unique, sovereign Self and Spirit.

Other Publications:

To order, send the appropriate amount plus $1.50 shipping to The Lorian Association at the address above. All books are perfect bound with a full color cover and include original art created for the publication.

Seeds of Inspiration: Deva Flower Messages
Dorothy Maclean
This lovely book chronicles Dorothy's connection with the intelligence of nature. It brings together for the first time most of her flower messages, truly *Seeds of Inspiration*. It includes several black and white flower illustrations. Perfect for daily meditations or giving a special gift.

$15.00 - 120 pages with introduction.

Great Glyph Silver Charm
3/4" diameter charm, a companion to **The Sidhe,** can be used as a small necklace or charm. $12.00.

The Sidhe: Wisdom from the Celtic Otherworld
John Matthews

This newest book by John traces his connection with a "Faery" or Sidhe being. It is full of wisdom and interesting detail about this "cousin" race to humanity. It includes six exercises and an illustration of a "Great Glyph" which acts as a tool of attunement with these graceful beings.

$15.00 - 120 pages plus preface.

The Story Tree
David Spangler

Over the years David has created several inspirational stories for family and friends. They are now available to everyone. Each embodies his unique spiritual insight and humanity. Most are based around Christmas themes and range from magical to mystical, science fiction to fantasy. All ages enjoy this wonderful collection.

$15.00 - 216 pages with illustrations.

Manifestation: Creating the life you love
David Spangler

Expanding on David's earlier book *Everyday Miracles* this evocative color illustrated deck and book gives ready access to the principles and application of shaping our personal and collective worlds. It will be valuable to anyone who would like to create a richer, fuller life; for themselves, for others and for our world.

$25.00 - 55 full color cards (2.5" X 3.5") with 88 page instruction manual.

"This book reminds me of words spoken by kind Cherokee elders regarding the entwined consciousness of trees and humanity. The text reads like a sermon calling the reader to recognize the sacredness of all life and the interdependence of human thoughts and actions with the environment. To remember that there is one mind underlying the appearances of individual egos is an antidote to separation and aggression.

"May each reader recall that just as trees offer life giving oxygen to the environment and the support of all beings on earth, our thoughts move through the atmosphere and give rise to the appearances and situations occurring on our planet. The message is of the bio-resonance of thoughts energizing physical expression, and the interdependence of all beings expressing the potential of the holy mystery which unites all.

"May this title benefit all beings and rekindle the memory that all is one in the dance of life."

Venerable Dhyani Ywahoo, Cherokee elder, Tibetan Buddhist teacher, and founder of Sunray Meditation Society, Sunray Peace Villiage, Lincoln, VT and Vajra Dakini Nunnery